This gymnastics goalbook belongs to:

_____

© Dream Co Publishing 2019. ISBN 978-0-9951238-3-0

Sports club bulk orders: orders@dreamcomedia.nz

Contents:

Info	page 1
Level/Badge Achievements	page 2
Encouraging Quotes	page 4
Term Gymnastics Goals	page 6
Weekly Class Goals	page 14

Fun Gymnastics Info:

Name: _____

Age: _____

Recreational level/Class: _____

Club: _____

Coach/es: _____

Favourite skill/s: _____

_____

Favourite apparatus/s: _____

_____

Favourite Olympic gymnast: _____

_____

Favourite gymnastics outfit:_____

Incentive Awards/Badges /Level Achievements

_____
_____
_____
_____
_____
_____
_____
_____
_____
_____
_____

Incentive Awards/Badges /Level Achievements

Favourite encouraging words or quotes:

_____

_____

_____

_____

_____

_____

_____

_____

_____

_____

_____

◇ *You can do it!* ◇

Favourite encouraging words or quotes:

_____

_____

_____

_____

_____

_____

_____

_____

_____

_____

_____

◇ *Go for gold!* ◇

 **My Term Gymnastics Goals:**

Date: _____

_____
_____
_____
_____
_____
_____
_____
_____
_____
_____
_____

 Dreams are possible.

My Term Gymnastics Outcomes:

Date: _____

_____
_____
_____
_____
_____
_____
_____
_____
_____
_____
_____
_____

◇ *Flipping out is fun!* ◇

 # My Term Gymnastics Goals:

Date: _____

_____

_____

_____

_____

_____

_____

_____

_____

_____

_____

 Don't give up!

My Term Gymnastics Outcomes:

Date: _____

_____
_____
_____
_____
_____
_____
_____
_____
_____
_____
_____
_____

◇ *Train like a champion.* ◇

 **My Term Gymnastics Goals:**

Date: _____

_____
_____
_____
_____
_____
_____
_____
_____
_____
_____
_____

 Aim high!

My Term Gymnastics Outcomes:

Date: _____

_____

_____

_____

_____

_____

_____

_____

_____

_____

_____

_____

_____

◇ *You're a star!* ◇

 **My Term Gymnastics Goals:**

Date: _____

_____

_____

_____

_____

_____

_____

_____

_____

_____

_____

_____

◇ *If you don't try – you won't know what you're actually capable of.* ◇

My Term Gymnastics Outcomes:

Date: _____

_____
_____
_____
_____
_____
_____
_____
_____
_____
_____
_____
_____

◇ *You got this!* ◇

 **My Weekly Class Goals:**

Date: _____

_____
_____
_____
_____
_____
_____
_____
_____
_____
_____
_____

 You're amazing.

My Weekly Class Outcomes:

Date: _____

_____

_____

_____

_____

_____

_____

_____

_____

_____

_____

◇ *Believe – achieve.* ◇

My Weekly Class Goals:

Date: _____

_____

_____

_____

_____

_____

_____

_____

_____

_____

_____

_____

 ...it's a gymnast thing.

My Weekly Class Outcomes:

Date: _____

_____
_____
_____
_____
_____
_____
_____
_____
_____
_____
_____

◇ *Be flexible, be strong. And smile!* ◇

 **My Weekly Class Goals:**

Date: _____

_____

_____

_____

_____

_____

_____

_____

_____

_____

_____

_____

_____

◇ *You can do it!* ◇

My Weekly Class Outcomes:

Date: _____

_____

_____

_____

_____

_____

_____

_____

_____

_____

_____

_____

◇   *Go for gold!*   ◇

My Weekly Class Goals:

Date: _____

_____

_____

_____

_____

_____

_____

_____

_____

_____

_____

 Dreams are possible.

My Weekly Class Outcomes:

Date: _____

_____
_____
_____
_____
_____
_____
_____
_____
_____
_____
_____

◇ *Flipping out is fun!* ◇

 **My Weekly Class Goals:**

Date: _____

_____

_____

_____

_____

_____

_____

_____

_____

_____

_____

_____

 Don't give up!

My Weekly Class Outcomes:

Date: _____

_____
_____
_____
_____
_____
_____
_____
_____
_____
_____
_____

Train like a champion.

 **My Weekly Class Goals:**

Date: _____

_____

_____

_____

_____

_____

_____

_____

_____

_____

_____

_____

 Aim high!

My Weekly Class Outcomes:

Date: _____

_____

_____

_____

_____

_____

_____

_____

_____

_____

_____

_____

◇ *You're a star!* ◇

My Weekly Class Goals:

Date: _____

_____

_____

_____

_____

_____

_____

_____

_____

_____

_____

 Gymnastics counts as flying.

My Weekly Class Outcomes:

Date: _____

_____
_____
_____
_____
_____
_____
_____
_____
_____
_____

◇ *I love gymnastics!* ◇

 **My Weekly Class Goals:**

Date: _____

_____

_____

_____

_____

_____

_____

_____

_____

_____

_____

_____

 If you don't try – you won't know what you're actually capable of.

My Weekly Class Outcomes:

Date: _____

_____
_____
_____
_____
_____
_____
_____
_____
_____
_____
_____

◇ *You got this!* ◇

My Weekly Class Goals:

Date: _____

_____

_____

_____

_____

_____

_____

_____

_____

_____

_____

 Tumbling, leaping, cartwheeling – fun!

My Weekly Class Outcomes:

Date: _____

_____
_____
_____
_____
_____
_____
_____
_____
_____
_____
_____
_____

◇ *Don't forget to have fun.* ◇

 **My Weekly Class Goals:**

Date: _____

_____
_____
_____
_____
_____
_____
_____
_____
_____
_____
_____
_____

 Run towards a challenge, not away from it.

My Weekly Class Outcomes:

Date: _____

_____

_____

_____

_____

_____

_____

_____

_____

_____

_____

◇ *Standing on your hands is fun.* ◇

 ## My Weekly Class Goals:

Date: _____

_____
_____
_____
_____
_____
_____
_____
_____
_____
_____
_____

 You're amazing.

My Weekly Class Outcomes:

Date: _____

_____

_____

_____

_____

_____

_____

_____

_____

_____

_____

_____

◇ *Believe – achieve.* ◇

My Weekly Class Goals:

Date: _____

_____
_____
_____
_____
_____
_____
_____
_____
_____
_____
_____
_____

 ...it's a gymnast thing.

My Weekly Class Outcomes:

Date: _____

_____

_____

_____

_____

_____

_____

_____

_____

_____

_____

_____

_____

◇ *Be flexible, be strong. And smile!* ◇

 **My Weekly Class Goals:**

Date: _____

_____
_____
_____
_____
_____
_____
_____
_____
_____
_____
_____
_____

 You can do it!

My Weekly Class Outcomes:

Date: _____

_____
_____
_____
_____
_____
_____
_____
_____
_____
_____
_____

◇ *Go for gold!* ◇

My Weekly Class Goals:

Date: _____

_____
_____
_____
_____
_____
_____
_____
_____
_____
_____
_____
_____

 Dreams are possible.

My Weekly Class Outcomes:

Date: _____

_____

_____

_____

_____

_____

_____

_____

_____

_____

_____

◇ *Flipping out is fun!* ◇

 **My Weekly Class Goals:**

Date: _____

_____
_____
_____
_____
_____
_____
_____
_____
_____
_____
_____
_____

◇ *Don't give up!* ◇

My Weekly Class Outcomes:

Date: _____

_____
_____
_____
_____
_____
_____
_____
_____
_____
_____
_____
_____

◇ *Train like a champion.* ◇

 **My Weekly Class Goals:**

Date: _____

_____
_____
_____
_____
_____
_____
_____
_____
_____
_____
_____
_____

 Aim high!

My Weekly Class Outcomes:

Date: _____

_____

_____

_____

_____

_____

_____

_____

_____

_____

_____

◇ *You're a star!* ◇

 **My Weekly Class Goals:**

Date: _____

_____

_____

_____

_____

_____

_____

_____

_____

_____

_____

_____

_____

_____

◇ *Gymnastics counts as flying.* ◇

My Weekly Class Outcomes:

Date: _____

_____
_____
_____
_____
_____
_____
_____
_____
_____
_____
_____
_____

◇ *I love gymnastics!* ◇

My Weekly Class Goals:

Date: _____

_____
_____
_____
_____
_____
_____
_____
_____
_____
_____
_____
_____
_____

 If you don't try – you won't know what you're actually capable of.

My Weekly Class Outcomes:

Date: _____

_____

_____

_____

_____

_____

_____

_____

_____

_____

_____

_____

_____

◇ *You got this!* ◇

 **My Weekly Class Goals:**

Date: _____

_____
_____
_____
_____
_____
_____
_____
_____
_____
_____
_____

◇ *Tumbling, leaping, cartwheeling – fun!* ◇

My Weekly Class Outcomes:

Date: _____

_____

_____

_____

_____

_____

_____

_____

_____

_____

_____

_____

◇ *Don't forget to have fun.* ◇

My Weekly Class Goals:

Date: _____

_____
_____
_____
_____
_____
_____
_____
_____
_____
_____
_____
_____

 Run towards a challenge, not away from it.

My Weekly Class Outcomes:

Date: _____

_____
_____
_____
_____
_____
_____
_____
_____
_____
_____
_____
_____

◇ *Standing on your hands is fun.* ◇

 **My Weekly Class Goals:**

Date: _____

_____
_____
_____
_____
_____
_____
_____
_____
_____
_____
_____
_____
_____
_____

 You're amazing.

My Weekly Class Outcomes:

Date: _____

_____

_____

_____

_____

_____

_____

_____

_____

_____

_____

_____

_____

◇ *Believe – achieve.* ◇

 **My Weekly Class Goals:**

Date: _____

_____

_____

_____

_____

_____

_____

_____

_____

_____

_____

_____

 ...it's a gymnast thing.

My Weekly Class Outcomes:

Date: _____

_____

_____

_____

_____

_____

_____

_____

_____

_____

_____

◇ *Be flexible, be strong. And smile!* ◇

 **My Weekly Class Goals:**

Date: _____

_____
_____
_____
_____
_____
_____
_____
_____
_____
_____
_____
_____

 You can do it!

My Weekly Class Outcomes:

Date: _____

_____

_____

_____

_____

_____

_____

_____

_____

_____

_____

_____

_____

◇ *Go for gold!* ◇

 **My Weekly Class Goals:**

Date: _____

_____

_____

_____

_____

_____

_____

_____

_____

_____

_____

_____

 Dreams are possible.

My Weekly Class Outcomes:

Date: _____

_____
_____
_____
_____
_____
_____
_____
_____
_____
_____
_____
_____
_____

◇ *Flipping out is fun!* ◇

My Weekly Class Goals:

Date: _____

_____
_____
_____
_____
_____
_____
_____
_____
_____
_____
_____
_____
_____

◇ *Don't give up!* ◇

My Weekly Class Outcomes:

Date: _____

_____

_____

_____

_____

_____

_____

_____

_____

_____

_____

_____

_____

_____

◇ *Train like a champion.* ◇

My Weekly Class Goals:

Date: _____

_____
_____
_____
_____
_____
_____
_____
_____
_____
_____
_____
_____
_____

◇ *Gymnastics counts as flying.* ◇

My Weekly Class Outcomes:

Date: _____

_____
_____
_____
_____
_____
_____
_____
_____
_____
_____
_____
_____
_____

◇ *I love gymnastics!* ◇

 **My Weekly Class Goals:**

Date: _____

_____

_____

_____

_____

_____

_____

_____

_____

_____

_____

 If you don't try – you won't know what you're actually capable of.

My Weekly Class Outcomes:

Date: _____

_____
_____
_____
_____
_____
_____
_____
_____
_____
_____
_____
_____

◇ *You got this!* ◇

 **My Weekly Class Goals:**

Date: _____

_____
_____
_____
_____
_____
_____
_____
_____
_____
_____
_____

 Tumbling, leaping, cartwheeling – fun!

My Weekly Class Outcomes:

Date: _____

_____
_____
_____
_____
_____
_____
_____
_____
_____
_____
_____

◇ *Don't forget to have fun.* ◇

My Weekly Class Goals:

Date: _____

_____
_____
_____
_____
_____
_____
_____
_____
_____
_____
_____
_____
_____
_____

 Run towards a challenge, not away from it.

My Weekly Class Outcomes:

Date: _____

_____
_____
_____
_____
_____
_____
_____
_____
_____
_____
_____
_____
_____

◇ *Standing on your hands is fun.* ◇

 **My Weekly Class Goals:**

Date: _____

_____
_____
_____
_____
_____
_____
_____
_____
_____
_____
_____
_____

 You're amazing.

My Weekly Class Outcomes:

Date: _____

_____
_____
_____
_____
_____
_____
_____
_____
_____
_____
_____

◇ *Believe – achieve.* ◇

 **My Weekly Class Goals:**

Date: _____

_____
_____
_____
_____
_____
_____
_____
_____
_____
_____
_____

 ...it's a gymnast thing.

My Weekly Class Outcomes:

Date: _____

_____

_____

_____

_____

_____

_____

_____

_____

_____

_____

_____

_____

_____

◇ *Be flexible, be strong. And smile!* ◇

 **My Weekly Class Goals:**

Date: _____

_____
_____
_____
_____
_____
_____
_____
_____
_____
_____
_____
_____

◇ *You can do it!* ◇

My Weekly Class Outcomes:

Date: _____

_____
_____
_____
_____
_____
_____
_____
_____
_____
_____
_____
_____
_____

◇ *Go for gold!* ◇

My Weekly Class Goals:

Date: _____

_____

_____

_____

_____

_____

_____

_____

_____

_____

_____

◇ *Dreams are possible.* ◇

My Weekly Class Outcomes:

Date: _____

_____

_____

_____

_____

_____

_____

_____

_____

_____

_____

_____

◇ *Flipping out is fun!* ◇

My Weekly Class Goals:

Date: _____

_____

_____

_____

_____

_____

_____

_____

_____

_____

_____

_____

 Don't give up!

My Weekly Class Outcomes:

Date: _____

_____

_____

_____

_____

_____

_____

_____

_____

_____

_____

_____

Train like a champion.

 **My Weekly Class Goals:**

Date: _____

_____

_____

_____

_____

_____

_____

_____

_____

_____

_____

_____

 Aim high!

My Weekly Class Outcomes:

Date: _____

_____
_____
_____
_____
_____
_____
_____
_____
_____
_____
_____
_____

◇ *You're a star!* ◇

My Weekly Class Goals:

Date: _____

_____
_____
_____
_____
_____
_____
_____
_____
_____
_____
_____
_____

◇ *Gymnastics counts as flying.* ◇

My Weekly Class Outcomes:

Date: _____

_____
_____
_____
_____
_____
_____
_____
_____
_____
_____
_____
_____

◇ *I love gymnastics!* ◇

 **My Weekly Class Goals:**

Date: _____

_____

_____

_____

_____

_____

_____

_____

_____

_____

_____

_____

 If you don't try – you won't know what you're actually capable of.

My Weekly Class Outcomes:

Date: _____

_____
_____
_____
_____
_____
_____
_____
_____
_____
_____
_____
_____
_____

◇ *You got this!* ◇

 **My Weekly Class Goals:**

Date: _____

_____
_____
_____
_____
_____
_____
_____
_____
_____
_____
_____
_____

 Aim high!

My Weekly Class Outcomes:

Date: _____

_____
_____
_____
_____
_____
_____
_____
_____
_____
_____
_____
_____

◇ *You're a star!* ◇

My Weekly Class Goals:

Date: _____

_____
_____
_____
_____
_____
_____
_____
_____
_____
_____
_____
_____

◇ *Gymnastics counts as flying.* ◇

My Weekly Class Outcomes:

Date: _____

_____
_____
_____
_____
_____
_____
_____
_____
_____
_____
_____

◇ *I love gymnastics!* ◇

 ## My Weekly Class Goals:

Date: _____

_____

_____

_____

_____

_____

_____

_____

_____

_____

_____

 Tumbling, leaping, cartwheeling – fun!

My Weekly Class Outcomes:

Date: _____

_____
_____
_____
_____
_____
_____
_____
_____
_____
_____
_____

◇ *Don't forget to have fun.* ◇

 **My Weekly Class Goals:**

Date: _____

_____

_____

_____

_____

_____

_____

_____

_____

_____

_____

_____

 Run towards a challenge, not away from it.

My Weekly Class Outcomes:

Date: _____

_____
_____
_____
_____
_____
_____
_____
_____
_____
_____
_____

◇ *Standing on your hands is fun.* ◇

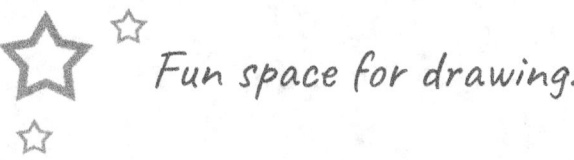
Fun space for drawing:

www.ingramcontent.com/pod-product-compliance
Lightning Source LLC
Chambersburg PA
CBHW070436010526
44118CB00014B/2066